HOW TO TIE A TIE

*the gentleman's guide
to the perfect knot*

STERLING
New York

STERLING
New York

An Imprint of Sterling Publishing Co., Inc.
1166 Avenue of the Americas
New York, NY 10036

STERLING
and the distinctive Sterling logo
are registered trademarks of
Sterling Publishing Co., Inc.

ISBN 978-1-4549-3132-4

Distributed in Canada by Sterling
Publishing Co., Inc., c/o Canadian
Manda Group, 664 Annette Street ▶
Toronto, Ontario, M6S 2C8, Canada
▶ Distributed in the United Kingdom
by GMC Distribution Services Castle
Place, 166 High Street, Lewes, East Sussex,
BN7 1XU, United Kingdom ▶ Distributed
in Australia by NewSouth Books, University of
New South Wales, Sydney, NSW 2052, Australia

For information about custom editions, special
sales, and premium and corporate purchases, please
contact Sterling Special Sales at 800-805-5489
or specialsales@sterlingpublishing.com.

Manufactured in China

2 4 6 8 10 9 7 5 3 1

sterlingpublishing.com

Cover design by David Ter-Avanesyan ▶ Interior design
by Christine Heun ▶ Photography by Christopher Bain ▶
Illustration by Mario Ferro and Alexis Seabrook ▶ Models:
Kevin Doherty, James Jayo, Gavin Motnyk ▶
For image credits, see page 121

CONTENTS

INTRODUCTION iv

A BRIEF HISTORY OF TIES 1

HOW TO CHOOSE A TIE 11

THE KNOTS

·ıl| |lı·

INTRODUCTION

Dressing well is a form of good manners.
Tom Ford

Knots mean business. They symbolize fertility, strength, unions, mystery, dilemmas, and solutions. A man in a tie means business, too—even if that business has nothing to do with commerce and everything to do with looking his best. If you're going to wear a tie, you need to be able to knot it properly.

The Ashley Book of Knots, published in 1944, describes approximately 4,000 different knots. In 1999, Thomas Fink and Yong Mao, theoretical physicists at Cambridge, determined that you can use almost 100 of them specifically to tie a tie. Mikael Vejdemo-Johansson of the KTH Royal Institute of Technology in Stockholm wrote a scholarly paper in 2014 showing that 177,147 ways to tie a tie exist. If you want to look put together, you need to know how to tie only a smart selection of that number, which appear in this book.

Tying a knot doesn't take long to learn, and once you've mastered the basics it's hard to forget how to do it correctly. Those basics come naturally enough, but they require practice for perfection. The more you do it, the better you get. Some men prefer using many different knots, while some stick with just one or two mainstays. Either way, it's good to know a few more—or have them handily at your fingertips in the pages that follow—so you can vary your style to suit different collars, occasions, or moods. You might like how one complements the shape of your chin or makes a bold knot from a thin tie. Some ties are best when you want to shine or when you don't want to draw undue attention to yourself.

A well-chosen, smartly worn tie stands as one of the pillars of a man's style, so it's important to get it right. After college, the average adult male

---

▶ A young Cary Grant looking dapper in a white bow tie.

dresses and undresses roughly 18,000 times. Depending on your profession, calling, or sartorial worldview, you may be choosing and knotting a veritable mountain of ties. But even if you're not a tie guy, consider the following: Job interviews, weddings, funerals, religious events, charity gatherings, and certain soirees all require the presence of a tie around your neck. The color of the tie itself can indicate the formality level of the event. Also consider: Both Cary Grant and James Bond looked superb in a bow tie.

Only Truman Capote, Tom Wolfe, and a few others could manage the tie as everyday apparel. Colonel Sanders somehow paired a string tie with a lifetime of southern-fried similes and parlayed himself into a fast-food luminary. Many a clammy gent sporting a clip-on, poly-blend necktie and a short-sleeve button-down shirt has stolen the show at a neighborhood social. Bond wouldn't be caught dead wearing either of these. Neither should you.

You're holding this handy little tome, so you know the importance of style and avoiding the sartorial misdemeanors described above. You already know what *not* to do. But in a post–casual Friday world, in which men's style often smacks of the agnostic, even some of the basic rules can prove elusive. What are the standard length and width for a tie? Can a prospective employer or mate, five feet away, tell the difference between a cheap tie and a good one? What's the best way to coordinate a tie's weave and width with suit fabrics and lapels? What knots go with which collars? What's proper tie etiquette?

In the following pages, you'll find answers to these questions along with all of the basic rules and regulations for the art of wearing ties—and how to break them if you choose. You'll also encounter fun facts, tidbits of encouragement and admonition, and lore and wisdom from style icons past and present. You won't find a lot of fashion fuss, just the must-know guidelines, along with a few finer points for looking good while wearing a tie. Because even if you're not gaming in Monte Carlo or skiing the Matterhorn, you want to look your best.

᛫ıǁ ǁı᛫

A BRIEF HISTORY OF TIES

There's never a new fashion but it's old.

Geoffrey Chaucer

Men have been donning neckwear for a very long time. The tie itself—known properly as a straight tie—is well-designed, orderly, and has clean lines. Its history, on the other hand, is loose and unkempt, with an indistinct point of origin and blurry development. If you never liked history class, skip ahead to the next section, How to Choose a Tie (page 11). But if you want to delve deeper into how and why we came to the practice of wrapping long strips of fabric around our necks, read on, good sir.

TIES TO WAR

Like many fashion trends—such as parkas, cargo pants, camouflage, and aviator sunglasses—the tie began as an article of military utility. In 1974, near Xi'an, the ancient capital of China, archaeologists unearthed the tomb of Qin Shih Huang (259–210 BC), the first Chinese emperor. In it,

they found a phalanx of some 7,500 terra-cotta soldiers, each with a knotted scarf or neckerchief around his neck. Before this discovery, historians had credited the Romans with inventing the tie, called a *focale*, citing the 2,500 or so soldiers wearing them on Trajan's Column, a war monument erected by Emperor Trajan in Rome in AD 113. In both cases, purely practical purposes prompted the usage. The tie absorbed sweat and protected soldiers' necks from the elements. Subsequent Chinese artifacts show no one wearing neckwear like this from the third century BC until the 1600s, when European style began influencing Chinese fashions. Roman soldiers continued to sport their *focalia* for a time, but, as the empire Christianized, ties disappeared from history for a millennium and a half.

The straight tie, as we know it, descends from the cravat, which came of age after the Thirty Years' War

▶ The terra-cotta warriors, discovered near the Chinese city of Xi'an, wore the world's first neckties.

(1618–1648). King Louis XIII of France hired a regiment of Croatian mercenaries to help his fight against the Holy Roman Empire. The Croatians wore knotted neckerchiefs, eventually called "cravats" (from the French word for Croatian), to keep their necks warm. The look of the cravat appealed to the French soldiers, who created their own version—a collar stiffly starched and pressed—but that proved cumbersome both to wear and to maintain. French military men carried the look back to the French court, where the fashion-conscious incorporated it into civilian style. Cravats then migrated from France to England with King Charles II, who returned from exile in King Louis XIV's court to England in 1660. At the same time, more sober cravats were sailing with the Puritans from England to the New World.

CRAVATS

The first civilian cravats consisted of lace or lace-edged muslin or cambric wrapped and knotted around the neck, the ends draping over the chest. By the end of the seventeenth century, those early cravats had become more or less required wear for gentlemen in Europe, the British Isles, and the American colonies. Men tied them in a variety of ways: simple knots fastened with smaller bits of fabric or ribbon; bows that grew to enormous, foppish proportions later called *lavalières*, after their adoption by the duchess of la Vallière, King Louis XIV's mistress; and a loose knot dubbed the Steinkirk for its debut at the 1692 Battle of Steenkerque in Flanders.

For the Steinkirk, legend has it that an English regiment's attack at dawn took French troops by surprise. In their haste to rally, the French abandoned their usually carefully tied cravats and instead loosely knotted their neckerchiefs, leaving one end hanging down. A more intentional variant of this, with ends entwined and one popped through a jacket's buttonhole, became a mainstay in England and Europe in the early eighteenth century and through that century's end in America.

Other forms of neckwear made their mark in the 1700s, most notably the stock, which, following tradition, began as a military style in France and what is now Germany. An almost absurdly simplified cravat, the stock at first consisted of a simple strip of folded plain white muslin fastened behind the neck. Its severe, choker-like design became a fad with young men who used it to signal their patriotism. With its popularity came additions and changes. Men often wore it with a frilly lace front piece, called a *jabot*, or rigged it in an arrangement with the eighteenth-century equivalent of a ponytail holder. A piece of black ribbon tying back the hair was wound around and bow-tied over the white stock, the complete look called a solitaire. Even with this fancier approach, the stock was a pretty tame adornment. The cravat hadn't seen its most elaborate incarnations yet.

▶ King Charles II of England brought the fashion of ties from France to England.

DRESSING FOR EXCESS

Every era has its sartorial rebellions and extremes of fashion. In the latter half of the 1700s, young gentlemen and other men of means often made a grand tour of Europe after completing their schooling. At this time, England gave rise to a movement of preposterously dressed young men who aped Italian style, which earned them the sobriquet of Macaronis (after the newfangled pasta they encountered in Italy).

These Macaronis took fashion to theatrical extremes, embellishing their outfits with jewels and extravagant needlework, wearing enormous white-powdered wigs, and wrapping their necks with impossibly huge, floppy, lacy, bow-tied white cravats. Across the Channel, reacting against the horrors of the Revolution and Reign of Terror, the French took up this stylistic excess and tried to outdo it. The Incroyables (Unbelievables), as they became known, wore cravats consisting of so much fabric that, once tied, the wearer almost couldn't turn his head! Across the Atlantic, America remained rather more restrained, as a famous ditty records:

> *Yankee Doodle went to town,*
> *a-riding on a pony,*
> *stuck a feather in his hat,*
> *and called it Macaroni.*

As the eighteenth century came to a close, the cravat changed form again, most often seen as a square of diagonally folded muslin knotted or tied into a bow of relatively modest scale.

George "Beau" Brummell—an English military man and friend of the prince regent (later King George IV)—brought the cravat to

▶ The Macaronis took fashion soaring to new heights.

peak status in the opening years of the 1800s, paving the way for the importance of the straight tie in daily wear. A dandy and savvy social climber, Brummell took fashion seriously, and his attention to matters of dress made him a supreme arbiter of taste. His regular outfit, which prefigured how menswear looks today, consisted of pants tucked into knee-high boots, shirt, vest, tailcoat, and a perfectly tied white cravat. Brummell reportedly tied *dozens* of cravats, while dressing, before selecting one that looked good enough for public viewing. Few men reached that level of obsession, but the act did become something of an art, complete with its own complex set of styles, codes, and meanings.

French and English publications of the period showcased an increasing number of knots for the cravat, and the choice of knot and the skill of tying it could signal a man's class or other social inclinations. In 1818, *Neckclothitania; or Tietania* offered more than a dozen trendy styles. Nine years later, *L'Art de Se Mettre Sa Cravate* proffered 32 knots for the cravat. Then, in 1830, *L'Art de la Toilette* threw down the gauntlet with a whopping 72 ways to tie a cravat.

PRACTICAL FASHION

Brummell and his cronies transformed the tie into a rich mode of self expression, but the trendsetters who came after him had other ideas about men's fashion. The buttoned-up morals and mores of the Victorian era (1837–1900) led to men's jackets closing higher at the neck, leaving little room

for fancy cravats tied in complex knots. The rise of industrialism also meant that more men needed practical neckwear that signified a sense of formality but didn't require much time to create in

▶ Beau Brummell took the cravat to the pinnacle of its popularity.

the morning or much maintenance during the day. Neckwear didn't vanish from fashion altogether, but the number of its permutations did consolidate.

In varying degrees, we still use the three most popular Victorian types of neckwear today. The modern bow tie descends, like a Darwinian victor, from the cravat, lavalière, and other historical examples of neckwear tied in a bow. As practicality required smaller ties, two versions—the Butterfly and the Bat Wing (page 52)—became standard. The ascot more or less derived its shape from a style of cravat in which a man wore a square piece of cloth with its ends crossed and fastened with a pin. We wear the modern ascot, slightly more oblong than its forefather, tied the same way (page 117). Both bow ties and ascots have held a place in contemporary formal menswear, and both have ventured, with varying degrees of success, into casual wear as well.

Which brings us to the straight tie that you know and love. Of the variations that have come and gone, the Four-in-Hand, also known as the long tie, has made the most lasting mark, surviving numerous adaptations and modifications over the decades. Named for a gentleman's club (which itself took its title from a horse carriage

whereby one driver could control four horses), the Four-in-Hand arose in the early to mid-1800s, became popular with young sporty Brits, and stuck. The first models—often lined with rough, heavy material, just long enough to tuck into a vest, and cut straight up and down—proved somewhat tricky to knot. Nevertheless, their simplicity and a shift in collar fashions from stiff and upright to softer and turned down kept them in widespread use. Necessity, ever the mother of invention, led to a broad range of tacks, pins, clips, and other accessories to prevent slippage and other sartorial blunders.

RESILIENT STYLE

As the Victorian era gave way to the Edwardian and Jazz ages, the tie was holding steady, but it badly needed a makeover. In 1924, Jesse Langsdorf, a New Yorker, patented a new design for the tie, which he called Resilient Construction. It created the tie from three separate pieces of fabric cut on the bias, or diagonal to the grain of the fabric. This new process produced neckwear that hung nicely when knotted. Patterns appeared orderly on the knotted tie. The tie also kept its shape better and

▶ Oscar Wilde knew the importance of a well-tied necktie.

longer. In the 1920s, as throughout most of history, silk reigned as the fabric of choice. Knit ties, which resurface every couple of decades, became trendy and appeared in a range of shapes, sizes, and styles: two-tone, reversible, tight, loose, and specialty-weave. Diagonal stripes and darker hues proved particularly fashionable, especially dark reds, purples, blues, browns, and blacks. Art Deco—streamlining the fractured geometry of Cubism and crystallizing at the International Exhibition of Modern Decorative and Industrial Arts in Paris in 1925—introduced new palettes and bold new patterns.

Hollywood glitz and glamour conquered the 1930s, as did the famous elegance of the prince of Wales (King Edward VIII in 1936 and then, after his abdication, the duke of Windsor). At the other end of society, gangsters also captured the popular imagination and influenced everyday fashion. These diverse inspirations resulted in a mix of tie styles ranging from tidy and conservative to flashy and wild. Ties came in silk, blended weaves, and increasingly rayon, which proved cheaper, easier to clean, and more resistant to tears. Solid ties had their place, as did eclectic prints, including checks of all sizes, stripes, and other patterns. By the late 1930s, new weaving techniques and fabrics allowed for more intricate and complicated prints, such as florals, animal prints, abstract and geometric designs, and stylized plumes and swirls. Novelty ties—featuring advertising slogans, for example—also originated at this time.

As the world marched inexorably to war again, economic restraint took precedence, having a huge impact on tie design and production. Requisitioned for making military

▶ Clark Gable favored narrow collars and small knots.

▶ Even Marlene Dietrich got in on the act.

▶ In the 1930s, the Prince of Wales became a fashion icon.

▶ Tie styles began to change significantly in the 1950s.

goods, manufacturers produced fewer ties, which left designers plenty of time to dream up a pantheon of new looks. After the war, colors and patterns expressed the celebratory exuberance of the day. Ties appeared in bright colors and increasingly wild patterns: bold contrasting vertical stripes; stylized petals, plumes, and birds; Western, tropical, Middle Eastern, or Asian motifs; and printed images of everything from playing cards and cowboys to flamingos and spaceships. In 1947, *Esquire* defined this as the

"bold look," which characterized the tie through the mid-1950s. Tie makers largely used rayon or Dacron with a wide range of new weaving techniques and printing methods, including hand painting, screen printing, and even photographic transfer. By the late 1950s, tastes trended more conservatively again, swinging to muted colors and tidier, narrower, often square-ended styles. The first leather ties also debuted.

Every age defines itself in part by resisting its immediate past, so the

▶ The 1980s brought tie fashions to new excesses, but here the members of Duran Duran rock more classic looks.

1960s spirit of flower-power rebellion rendered ties unfashionable because they represented traditional authority. The fashion trends of that decade took their cues from hippie counterculture. Ties grew farcically wide. Colors became vivid and often gaudy. Prints reverted to nature and came in a variety of international patterns. The anti-tie movement gained more traction in the 1970s, but that decade of economic turmoil also gave rise to the "kipper" tie, up to six inches wide, and revived the leather tie, now in a plethora of outlandish colors, which held sway into the 1980s. Simplifying the past, the skinny tie became popular in the 1980s, as did a range of boldly contrasting colors and patterns. Also in

the greedy '80s, Hermès, originally a harness and bridle producer and now a fashion house, launched its signature pattern of small repeated animal motifs, a style that remains elegant and whimsical but well within the bounds of convention.

Annual tie sales in America, the world's largest market, peaked in 1995 at $1.8 billion for a staggering 100 million ties. As the workplace dress code has devolved since then from professional to business casual to casual, fewer men are wearing ties to work, and just 6 percent wear a tie to the office every day. Nevertheless, while widths, lengths, styles, colors, and patterns may change radically over time, the smart, sound architecture of the tie endures.

HOW TO CHOOSE A TIE

A man is worth as much as his tie.

Honoré de Balzac

If your professional life doesn't mandate that you sport a tie on a daily basis, then you've probably worn one for a job interview or other special occasion. If you haven't yet, you soon will—and you'll need a tie that looks good, lasts, meshes with a variety of styles, and expresses a piece of your identity.

Jackets, pants, and shirts come in a limited range of colors, so a tie offers a golden opportunity to achieve fashion distinction. Stores often stock a dizzying array of ties, though, making it feel daunting to choose the right one. The right tie can seal the deal, but the wrong tie can make you look garish and gauche. Thankfully selecting the right tie can be an easy, inexpensive way to pull together any look, whether casual, professional, or formal.

In the pages that follow, you'll learn how to determine the quality of a tie. At best, a poor quality tie won't knot properly or hang well, and it will fray and fade quickly because

cheap ties look and act, well, *cheap*. At worst, a cheap tie will cost you an interview callback or a second date. Quality ties last longer, have classic patterns that look better, and pair well with different combinations of shirts, jackets, and suits. The best ties do cost the most, but you don't have to spend lavishly for quality. Various producers make a wide range of ties that are well constructed, handsome, and reasonably priced. By heeding the information that follows, you can discern which ties are worth buying and which to avoid.

HAND

A tie's type and quality of fabric, combined with the method and condition of its construction and production, determine its hand, or tactility. Overall weight, texture, volume, and fall (how it hangs) establish the hand, and a fine tie is said to have a good hand. When you pick it up and lay it across your palm, it feels nicely substantial. As with a fine wine, the impression of balance lingers. If you're not sure what that means, try this: Hold a mass-produced, synthetic tie in your hand, then immediately replace it with a handmade, 100 percent silk tie. The difference will surprise you. It's the tactile equivalent of sipping a jug wine and then a fine Bordeaux. If you become familiar with how the hands of different ties feel, starting with the ones that you already own, you'll understand the quality of each tie you consider adding to your wardrobe.

CONSTRUCTION

How the manufacturer sews the parts of a tie together is as important as the parts themselves, and you'll learn more about this when we give you four foolproof quality tests (page 26) to run on prospective ties to make sure they do the job right.

Like a Manhattan, a good tie has three main parts, one that shows and two that don't. When you're wearing a tie, the part that shows is the **shell** or envelope (external fabric), often sewn together from three or more smaller pieces of fabric, which you can spot by the **seam** between each piece. Together these form the **blade** (wide end), the **neck** (middle), and the **tail** (narrow

end). The carefully curved but not creased fabric where the shell goes from the front to the back of the tie is called the **rolled edge**. The back of the shell often contains two pieces of fabric: the **keeper loop**, usually created from the same fabric as the shell, and the label, often made of silk or acetate. When you're done knotting a tie, you slide the tail through the keeper loop to keep it from showing. (You can slide it through the producer's label as well for extra stability.) Below these structural components, a tie also has a bar tack, a thick stitch that unites the two sides of the shell and stabilizes the slip stitch within. Sometimes a bar tack appears on the tail-end of the tie as well. At the bottom of the blade and tail, you can see the **tipping** of the tie. If the tipping looks different from the fabric of the shell or lining, it's called decorative. If it looks the same, it's called self-tipping. The hem connects the tipping to the shell. The **margin** is the fabric between the tipping and the edge of the blade. Often stitched into the tail, a **care and origin tag** indicates the tie's place of manufacture, production materials, and how to clean it.

The parts that don't show consist of the **lining** and the **interlining**. The interlining, made of heavier fabric

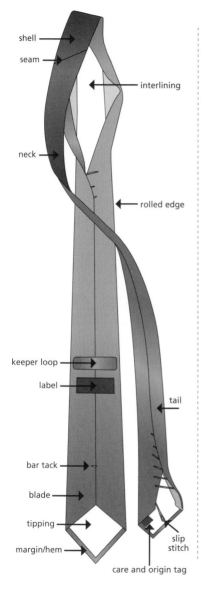

shell

seam

interlining

neck

rolled edge

keeper loop

label

tail

bar tack

blade

tipping

margin/hem

slip stitch

care and origin tag

sewn into the shell, serves as the tie's skeleton. A 100 percent silk tie lined with silk and interlined with muslin has the best hand.

Inside the shell, one bit of absolutely crucial stitching merits special attention. The **slip stitch** runs the full length of the tie, holding it together, giving it what's called "play," keeping it elastic and properly shaped, and thwarting damage from repeated knotting and unknotting. Why such a big deal? The slip stitch can be made only by hand, indicating that your tie—even if commercially manufactured—is hand-finished. You may have to poke beneath the shell to see it, but make sure to do this. Spot the slip stitch and you know that you're holding a quality garment.

FABRIC

Ties can consist of a variety of natural or manmade fabrics, including silk, wool, cotton, leather, rayon, polyester, and various blends. A tie's fabric is important not just for its weight and texture but also for how it incorporates and maintains color and pattern. Synthetics are inexpensive, easier to clean, and have short-term durability, and they usually feature lower-quality colors, patterns, and designs. Stick with natural fibers, and you'll be in good shape. Let's take a closer look.

Natural Fibers

SILK

The absolute best material for a tie is 100 percent silk, which gives a tie the best hand. Three factors determine the weight of silk: number of threads (which themselves consist of many tinier silk filaments), thickness, and weight. Certain manufacturing processes and types of dyes also affect the silk weight. The weave of silk makes it pleasant to touch and gives the fabric an elasticity that helps the final garment keep its shape. Silk weight is given in Japanese units of measure called momme (MAHM-mee). One momme weighs 3.75 grams, and tie silk generally weighs between 10 and 45 momme per square yard. Silk comes in a huge number of stunning colors and can incorporate any motif or pattern. Most silk ties fall into one of two major categories: woven and printed.

> **FUN FACT**
> It takes 110 silkworms to make the 245,000 feet of silk that go into one silk tie.

WOVEN SILK

The tie connoisseur wears only woven-silk ties. All silk fabric is woven, but in this case the manufacturer weaves the pattern, using differently colored threads, directly into the tie itself. As a result, patterns and motifs look sharp, and colors appear rich and vivid. Woven-silk ties feel best, hang best, and look best.

The textures of woven-silk ties vary a great deal. Some special-order ties use extremely expensive, highly specialized textures such as pleated, flocked, or watered silk. Satin weave creates a superbly smooth, feather-soft, lustrous fabric. Unusual weaves, such as a flecked crepe, basket weave, or a combination, can produce beautiful ties of complex craftsmanship. Certain manufacturers specialize in creating these multi-weave masterpieces. If you own woven-silk ties, they most likely feature a plain weave, the texture used for crepe, faille, ottoman, and rep fabrics.

PRINTED SILK

Like their fancier woven brothers, printed silk ties offer a wide range of attractive colors and patterns. As a rule, their designs don't look as sophisticated, but they have one big advantage: They cost notably less. This

TIE CHART

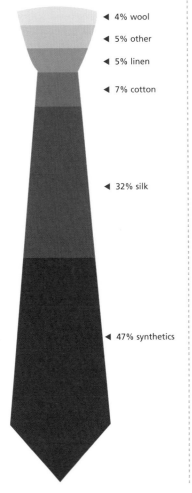

◄ 4% wool

◄ 5% other

◄ 5% linen

◄ 7% cotton

◄ 32% silk

◄ 47% synthetics

winning combination of quality and affordability makes the printed-silk tie the most popular. Unless you're already a grabatologist—more on that later—most of your ties probably consist of printed silk.

Manufacturers most often use a twill weave for printed silk ties and apply the pattern or motifs, color by color, by silk-screening. Strategically placed blocks obstruct the screen to ensure that one color passes through in exactly the desired location and nowhere else. One printed-silk tie may require anywhere from four or five screens—the most common number—and up to 25. The number of colors used directly influences the cost of manufacturing, so printed silk ties with many hues can cost quite a lot.

KNITTED SILK

Very fashionable in the 1970s but now an anomaly, the knitted-silk tie—usually a solid color with a square-finished end—can make for an interesting look if paired stylishly with the right shirt and jacket. Machines knit the silk of this tie, which feels slightly nubby and somewhat slippery in a fun and unusual way. Mastering the knitted-silk tie requires having a clearly defined flair for apparel. If at all in doubt, steer clear.

SILK BLENDS

POPLIN Like pure silks, poplin—a blend of silk and wool with the silk on the surface and wool on the underside—makes a great tie fabric. Their unique weave makes poplin ties both sumptuous and sturdy, with a wonderful hand, particularly when the wool is cashmere. Like woven silks, they cost a bit more, but their quality of construction and impressive shelf life make them worth the expense.

OTHER BLENDS Manufacturers can blend silk with various natural fibers to produce lightweight fabrics that make great ties for warmer seasons and climes. Sometimes they blend it with linen or mogadore, a tightly woven mix of silk and cotton. Once in a while, they add a smidgen of polyester to increase a tie's elasticity. Again, these fabrics aren't cheap, but they do last, making them economical in the long run.

SPECIAL-EFFECTS SILK

Producers can treat silk in a number of ways to create extremely luxe fabrics with unusual, sophisticated effects. Pleated silk, washed silk (roughened with sand or pebbles), moiré (crushed) and gum silk (a denser, velvety texture) all make stunning ties for more formal occasions.

OTHER NATURAL FIBERS
COTTON

Cotton ties come in lots of colors and patterns. They cost less than silk but more than synthetics. Cotton is dye-fast, so the color quality dazzles, making it quite pleasing as a tie fabric. As with silk, you can wear a cotton tie year-round with casual wear and in summer for dressier occasions. A cotton tie doesn't feel as good as silk or a silk blend, however.

SEERSUCKER This lightweight cotton fabric has stripes of alternating density, making it look relaxed and slightly wrinkled. The name comes from the Persian words *sheer* and *shakar,* which mean "milk" and "sugar," describing the smooth and rough textures of the stripes. Seersucker ties aren't all that common and are suited best for more casual summer events, such as an outdoor wedding.

CAMBRIC Named for the French town of Cambrai, Cambric is a light yet dense fabric originally made of linen but now made primarily of cotton. Not to be confused with Chambray, which is a weaving method, like denim. You won't find many ties made of cambric.

Linen

Cotton

Poplin

Wool

Leather

Silk

LINEN

Made from the flax plant, linen fabric absorbs moisture and dries faster than cotton, so it stays remarkably cool and fresh in hot, humid climates. Like seersucker, linen ties are rare and should be worn primarily to accompany a linen jacket or suit in hotter weather.

WOOL

Knitted or woven, wool ties wear well and can look marvelous. Like the knitted-silk tie, the knitted wool tie—of a single color and with square ends—had its heyday in the 1960s and 1970s, but it still makes the occasional appearance on the man with the right panache. In *From Russia with Love*, Sean Connery as James Bond made the black knitted tie look great with dark suits and crisp white shirts.

Woven-wool ties consist of high-end materials. Their heavier weight and cozier textures suit them particularly for winter ensembles. Tweed makes for an interesting albeit rare tie, too—and not for everyday wear. A tweed tie worn smartly with a spruce wool or tweed jacket can make an interesting departure from your usual cold-weather fare.

FELT When you apply hot water, agitation, and compression to wool, you make felt, a denser, slightly spongy version of the fabric. Felt breathes less than regular wool, so it's appropriate for particularly cold climates. Felt ties verge dangerously close to the novelty category, however, so tread carefully and conservatively with ties made of this material.

LEATHER

A few fashion houses make handsome ties in leather or suede, and some stylish men, who want an edgy casual look that plays with formality, look great in them. Leather ties skyrocketed in popularity during the late 1970s and early 1980s, but these days their novelty factor relegates them primarily to leather-centric events or locations.

Synthetic Fibers

Ties made of rayon, polyester, and synthetic blends are inexpensive, easy to maintain, and come in a Technicolor explosion of designs, colors, and patterns. Don't wear them.

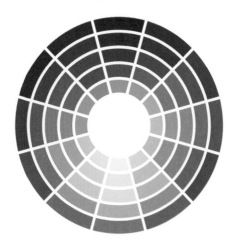

COLOR

Until the first half of the nineteenth century, the cravat and its cousins invariably appeared in white. Then, in the 1840s, black, somber and powerful, became the de rigueur color. Hues remained relatively dark for more than a century, when, in the 1950s, paler shades began to infiltrate the acceptable spectrum. Today you can buy a tie in nearly every color known to man.

Good ties come in many colors. The better the tie, the richer and more lush the color—and that's not a minor detail; it's critical. You don't have to develop Rothko-level skills for color theory, but it helps to know what shades suit your complexion, wardrobe, and personality. When it comes to color, the main challenge is which tie to wear with which shirt and then which jacket. First let's start with the color wheel.

Warm colors—reds, oranges, yellows—appear on the left and cool colors—greens, blues, purples—on the right. You can use the color wheel to help you choose the right color scheme with three simple rules: the principle of families, the principle of complements, and the principle of opposites. The principle of families minimizes contrast and helps create an overall theme, such as baby blue, royal blue, and navy blue all in a row. The principle of complements strikes a harmonious balance between colors, such as red and orange next to each other. The principle of opposites enhances contrast, such as yellow and purple side by side.

Contrast

First consider your complexion and your own natural contrast levels.

CONTRAST MATRIX

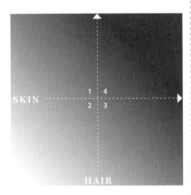

1. Lighter skin + darker hair: high contrast
2. Lighter skin + lighter hair: low contrast

3. Darker skin + lighter hair: high contrast
4. Darker skin + darker hair: low contrast

Men with low contrast levels will look best when wearing lighter hues and staying in single-color families. Men with high contrast levels should wear suits, shirts, and ties that maintain that stronger contrast. These guidelines offer a starting point for mixing and matching colors. If you're not sure, failsafe neutrals, such as tan, gray, and black, will give you the most versatility.

PATTERN

A pattern consists of a recurring motif. The better the tie, the crisper or more intricate the pattern—and you want to err on the side of subtlety. Smaller, less obtrusive patterns always look classier and more timeless.

CLUB

For the blueblood and the social aspirant alike, this pattern makes for an obvious choice. Emblazoned with the insignia of your preferred organization, the club tie offers a subtle yet fashionable way to project your personality. Never fake a club affiliation, though, which could cause offense or derision.

CUSTOM
Some ties employ an unconventional pattern or motif that doesn't repeat. As always, choose a classic, timeless look rather than anything outlandish.

DOTTED
As with other patterns, the smaller the dot, the more formal the look. Avoid larger dots, which will make you look like a clown.

FLORAL
Animal and flower prints present the greatest challenge in tie fashion. On the one hand, when done right, they can make a powerful statement. On the other hand, they're incredibly easy to get wrong and slide swiftly toward novelty.

GEOMETRIC
If you want to signify orderly intelligence and good design sense, this is the tie for you. Just take care to avoid a pattern that looks like the kitchen floor. A smaller pattern is always a safe bet.

PAISLEY
Named for the Scottish town that famously created designs imitating the Persian curved teardrop motif, this pattern evokes either international refinement or 1960s psychedelia. Choose wisely.

PLAID
This catchall category covers any pattern consisting of parallel and/ or overlapping perpendicular lines of the same or varying widths. It includes gingham, glen, graph check, madras, pin check, shepherd's check, tartan, tattersall, and windowpane. Because the lines naturally create visual contrast, it's best to wear plaid ties in light or pastel hues, particularly in spring.

RIBBON
This pattern usually follows the standard direction of a stripe, but in narrow lines.

STRIPES
The most basic tie pattern remains one of the most fashionable. Whether uniform and diagonal or tricolored and varying in width, a striped tie makes a dependable choice for all occasions.

Club

Dotted

Floral

Geometric

Paisley

Plaid

▶ HOW TO TIE A TIE ◀

Stripes

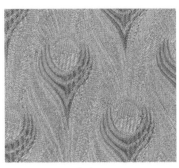

Custom

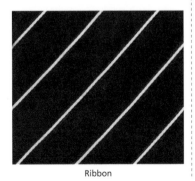

Ribbon

OTHER MOTIFS

The list of potential themes runs long, but a few offenders make regular appearances.

ART TIES

This category includes motifs or patterns from famous works of art and garments designed by famous artists. You can find the former most often in museum gift shops and catalogs. Bold, bleary-eyed Impressionism tends to rule the roost, although it's easy enough to find ties with images of anything from Renaissance art and Cubism to Surrealism and Pop Art. Specimens with subtler motifs or images occasionally look good, but in general it's best to avoid these sartorial manifestos.

The Italian Futurists dabbled in creating various eccentric, colorful ties. In the 1940s, Salvador Dalí also produced ties for sale. Artists can and do create beautiful neckties. Just mind the not-so-fine line between terrific and terrifically tacky.

SPORTS TIES

The English love ties with motifs drawn from hunting, riding, golfing, fishing, and other traditionally upper-class leisure activities that take place in the great outdoors. Feel free to wear fine ties featuring those and other subtle sports patterns—miniature tennis rackets, polo players, or the like—in casual contexts that allow for their boyish effect. Dodge any tie that shrieks your allegiance to a particular sport, team, or player.

NOVELTY TIES

Never express wit or humor on or with a tie. Avoid cartoon characters, equations, handwriting, lights, logos, maps, musical instruments, national flags, keyboards, slogans, and other fashion abominations.

DIMENSIONS

A quality tie will have the right dimensions already, but fashions change quickly. Ties grow wider or skinnier, longer or shorter, depending on the decade. To stand the test of time, a tie should measure:

- 3¼ to 3½ inches wide at the widest point
- If you need a quick way to measure the width of a tie, use a $1 bill. If the tie reaches the *right* side of Washington's face, it's the *right* width.
- 55 to 56 inches long

HANDMADE TIES

Producers can make ties almost wholly by machine, by machine with hand finishing, or completely by hand. Machine-manufactured ties with hand finishing account for the greatest percentage of quality ties on the market, so that's what you probably have in your wardrobe now. Manufacturers create many garments of each design, which makes them affordable, well constructed, and attractive. If you want a true work of craftsmanship, here are your other options.

Tie artisans ply their trade in small studios, producing limited editions of particular designs. They pay superbly careful attention to all stages of construction, thereby creating top-of-the-line garments. As with all quality goods, their wares can cost a great deal. But if you care for them well, they'll last a lifetime and likely still be in good enough shape to hand down to a son or nephew. A word to the wise, however: "Handmade" on the label doesn't necessarily mean handmade. Many foreign companies ship boatloads of machine-manufactured ties across the globe, where garment workers add the "handmade" label (as though the label itself justified its false message). In other words, know your vendor.

Bespoke Ties

Some boutique haberdashers and fashion houses, largely in Europe, still offer custom services. A man may decide to have a tie custom made because he has particular requirements or preferences with regard to the designs of standard ties. Most often, the request for a custom-made tie comes from a man who's significantly taller, shorter, or broader than average. Some esoteric knots and certain shirt collars also require bespoke ties.

> **FUN FACT**
> The Satya Paul Design Studio made fashion history when they partnered with the Suashish Diamond Group to create a pure silk tie containing 271 diamonds and 150 grams of gold. The Suashish Necktie cost $220,000, making it the most expensive tie in the world.

TESTING FOR QUALITY

Now that you know all of the factors that go into a quality tie, you need to know how to put that knowledge into action when deciding whether to buy a particular tie. As a reminder, a worthwhile tie has:

- heavy hand
- good elasticity
- full lining
- hand-stitching with a slip stitch
- diagonal grain

To determine whether a tie is good, here are four tests you can administer to the garment:

Twist Test
Drop the tie from its narrow end and make sure that it falls without twisting.

Center Test
Place the middle of the tie over your forearm. The narrow end should center against the wide end.

Elasticity Test
Give the tie a good yank at both ends. It should return to its original shape right away.

Stitch Test
Make sure the lining is stitched securely to the external fabric and that it doesn't shift or slide over when you pull it. Look at the seams that secure the lining to the tie and make sure that they're strong and that they extend far enough upward to conceal the interlining. Under the back seam of the external fabric, confirm that the tie has a slip stitch, which will allow the tie to maintain its elasticity and shape over time.

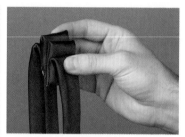

Twist

Center

Elasticity

Stitch

THE KNOTS

ᵼᵼᵎᵼ ᵼᵼᵼᵼ

The Kent

SKILL LEVEL ▼ ▽ ▽ ▽ ▽
NUMBER OF STEPS *3*

HOW TO WEAR IT

YOUR BUILD SMALLER
COLLAR WIDTH NARROWER
FABRIC DENSITY THICKER
TIE LENGTH SHORTER

Sometimes called the simple knot or the Oriental because of its popularity in China, the Kent is small, perfectly symmetrical, and easy to learn. Men rarely use it in the West, however. Give it a try as a polite nod to Chinese culture or as a simpler, subtle variation of the Four-in-Hand. The Kent's smaller size makes it a good option for a shorter tie or a taller man because the smallness of the finished knot ensures more fabric length at the end.

NOTE Begin with the tie wrapped inside out, seam showing, around your neck.

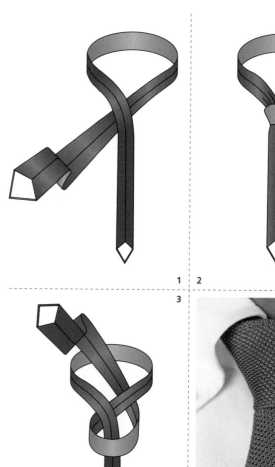

1 **2**

3

② The Prince Albert

SKILL LEVEL ▼ ▽ ▽ ▽ ▽

NUMBER OF STEPS 5

HOW TO WEAR IT

YOUR BUILD SMALLER

COLLAR WIDTH NARROWER

FABRIC DENSITY THICKER

TIE LENGTH SHORTER

Queen Victoria's consort died in 1861, before the Four-in-Hand gained popularity, so the Prince Albert takes its name in honor of the man rather than for how he wore his ties. This configuration slightly modifies the Four-in-Hand with an extra loop. This knot has a little more bulk and shortens the tie accordingly, making it a great option for shorter men. Ties made of softer, more malleable fabrics work best with this knot. In the last step, the active end of the tie goes through *both* horizontal loops, giving the finished look an extra edge and making you feel regal. Pull it tight to give it a tidy, slender look.

NOTE Don't use a tie with a satin finish because the fabric will slip and obscure the knot's special effect.

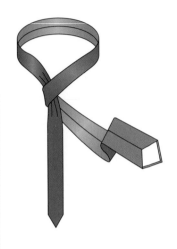

1

4

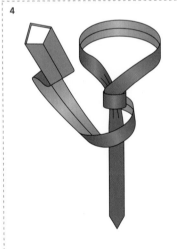

2

3

5

The Four-in-Hand

SKILL LEVEL ▼ ▽ ▽ ▽ ▽
NUMBER OF STEPS 5

HOW TO WEAR IT

YOUR BUILD	SMALLER
COLLAR WIDTH	NARROWER
FABRIC DENSITY	THICKER
TIE LENGTH	SHORTER

In the early nineteenth century, a new horse carriage design allowed one driver to control four horses simultaneously. The carriage became known as a four-in-hand, and a gentleman's driving club of the same name formed in 1856. The name of this knot probably derives from the neckwear of that group. The forerunner of the straight tie appeared then as well, and for a time both the tie and the knot went by the same name. The Four-in-Hand knot stuck because of the ease of tying it and its tidy finished look. The burgeoning ranks of middle-class men had to wear ties to work every day but didn't want to fuss with more complicated configurations. Gentlemen also wanted something simpler to wear for leisure pursuits, such as sports and travel. Until the 1930s, when the Windsor knot came into fashion, the Four-in-Hand reigned supreme, and it remains a menswear standard to this day.

It doesn't require lots of steps that eat a tie's final length, so it's great for taller men, and its slender, charmingly asymmetrical shape complements and downplays a rounder face. It works best with small-spread or tab collars.

1 | **2**

3

4 | 5

▶ HOW TO TIE A TIE ◀

The Kelvin

SKILL LEVEL ▼ ▽ ▽ ▽ ▽
NUMBER OF STEPS **6**

HOW TO WEAR IT

YOUR BUILD	SMALLER
COLLAR WIDTH	NARROWER
FABRIC DENSITY	THICKER
TIE LENGTH	SHORTER

Named in honor of William Thomson (Baron Kelvin), a physicist and early proponent of knot theory, the Kelvin modifies the Kent configuration with an extra step that gives the finished look slightly more volume and symmetry.

NOTE: Begin with the tie wrapped inside out, seam showing, around your neck.

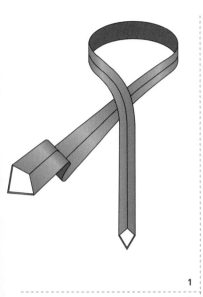

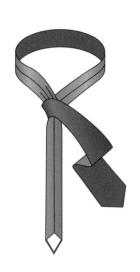

1

2

3

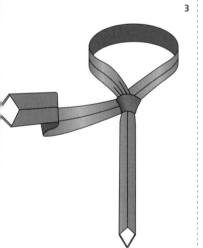

▶ HOW TO TIE A TIE ◀

The Pratt

SKILL LEVEL ▼ ▼ ▼ ▼ ▼

NUMBER OF STEPS **6**

HOW TO WEAR IT

YOUR BUILD **SMALLER**

COLLAR WIDTH **AVERAGE**

FABRIC DENSITY **THICKER**

TIE LENGTH **SHORTER**

In 1989, the *New York Times* broke the news of the discovery of a new knot in Minneapolis. Jerry Pratt, a retired U.S. Chamber of Commerce official and a nonagenarian, had been tying his ties in a particular way for decades. On a visit to the studio of WCCO-TV, Pratt showed Don Shelby, an anchor of the local news show, his novel way of tying a tie so it created a balanced, symmetrical knot—and it really was news. Even the Neckwear Association of America didn't know about it. The media wrongly dubbed this new knot the Shelby, although in actuality it derives from the Nicky and American men had been wearing it, as the Reverse Half-Windsor, since the 1940s. If you like your finished ties to have an elegant symmetry, this is the knot for you.

NOTE: Begin with the tie wrapped inside out, seam showing, around your neck.

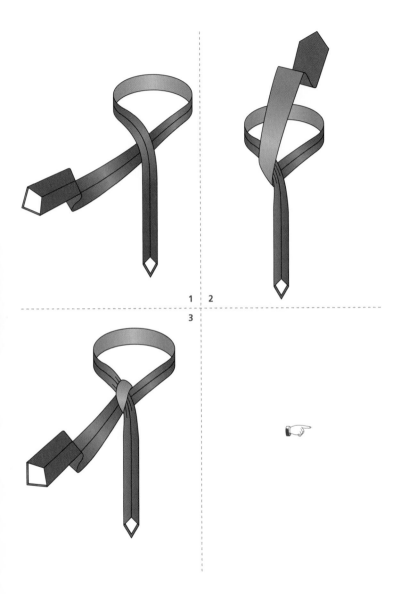

1 2
3

4 | 5

6

The Nicky

SKILL LEVEL ▼ ▼ ▼ ▼ ▼
NUMBER OF STEPS 6

HOW TO WEAR IT

YOUR BUILD	AVERAGE
COLLAR WIDTH	MEDIUM
FABRIC DENSITY	AVERAGE
TIE LENGTH	AVERAGE

In 1952, Leopoldo Curami—brother-in-law of John Nicky Chini, the founder of the Nicky tie shop in Milan—invented this knot, which finally appeared in book form in 1985. A few years later, Englishman David Kelsall accidentally tied the Pratt the wrong way and found himself holding the Nicky instead. This classic look goes well with lots of different face shapes, tie types, and shirt collars.

NOTE: Begin with the tie wrapped inside out, seam showing, around your neck.

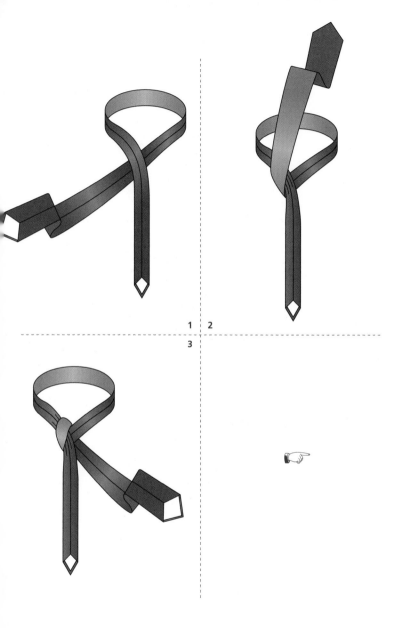

1 | 2
3

4 | 5

6

The Diagonal

SKILL LEVEL ▼ ▼ ▼ ▼ ▼

NUMBER OF STEPS 6

HOW TO WEAR IT

YOUR BUILD AVERAGE

COLLAR WIDTH MEDIUM

FABRIC DENSITY AVERAGE

TIE LENGTH AVERAGE

This modification of the Kelvin creates an eye-catching diagonal line in the finished knot. You want the architecture of the knot to shine, though, so use this configuration only with solid-color ties. (Patterns of any kind will look messy and discombobulated.) Wear this knot to less formal occasions that still require a touch of formality or when you want to show off a little bit.

1 | 2

3

4 | 5

6

The Bow Tie

SKILL LEVEL ▼ ▼ ▼ ▼ ▼

NUMBER OF STEPS **6**

HOW TO WEAR IT
YOUR BUILD ALL

COLLAR WIDTH NARROWER

FABRIC DENSITY AVERAGE

TIE LENGTH AVERAGE

At the end of the nineteenth century, the bow tie existed in various iterations: stiff, floppy, geometric, loopy, off-center, and so on. Then, in 1904, the Butterfly variant appeared and conquered the scene. The Bat Wing version runs smaller, has pointed ends, and ties more narrowly than the Butterfly. The least common version still worn today is called the straight or Thistle bow tie, the smallest and narrowest of the three, which has ends extending straight out on either side.

Bow ties don't dangle, fall forward, or get in the way, which explains why doctors and scientists favor them. Bow ties are lightweight and cover a smaller area of the body than straight ties, so they make a cooler option in hotter weather. Proceed with caution, however. They can and will set you apart from the crowd. Great men and fools alike have made them emblematic of their endeavors—with little middle ground between the two camps.

For casual wear, a bow tie works best with a button-down shirt with a straight point collar. The Thistle bow tie is just for casual wear. You can don the Butterfly or Bat Wing for casual or formal looks. Wear only the Butterfly for black-tie or white-tie events.

FUN FACT

Less than 1 percent of American men know how to tie a bow tie.

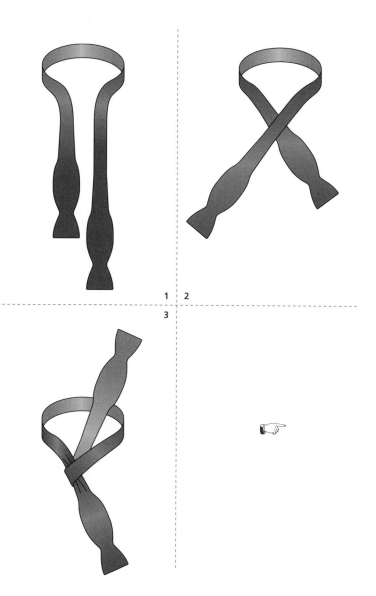

1 2
3

4 | 5

6

9

The Atlantic

SKILL LEVEL ▼ ▼ ▼ ▼ ▼
NUMBER OF STEPS 6

HOW TO WEAR IT
YOUR BUILD AVERAGE
COLLAR WIDTH MEDIUM
FABRIC DENSITY AVERAGE
TIE LENGTH AVERAGE

This unusual knot reverses aspects of the Pratt and Nicky and appears totally different from both. Use it for when you want to do something a little bit different for a fun, less formal occasion or when you want to show a little bit of extra personality. Because of the geometry of the final knot, avoid stripes or any kind of pattern and stick with a single-color tie.

NOTE: In the last step, pull the *blade* to tighten the final knot.

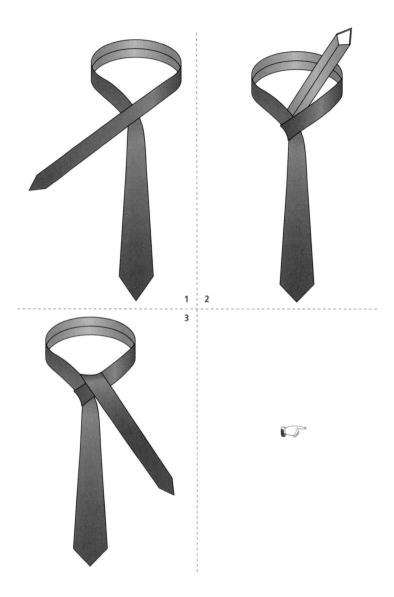

4 | 5

6

The Half-Windsor

SKILL LEVEL ▼ ▼ ▼ ▽ ▽
NUMBER OF STEPS 7

HOW TO WEAR IT

YOUR BUILD AVERAGE
COLLAR WIDTH MEDIUM
FABRIC DENSITY AVERAGE
TIE LENGTH AVERAGE

This knot isn't a variation of the Windsor, nor is it half as big—but you definitely should include it in your repertoire. In regular use since the 1950s, it makes a great everyday knot. Medium-sized and perfectly symmetrical, it suits various face shapes, a variety of tastes, and almost any type of shirt collar. Use it with a lightweight tie and you'll get a modest look. Tie a heavier tie with it and you'll get a little more volume.

NOTE: As you tighten the tie in step seven, gently press a finger below the knot to create a tiny indentation or "dimple."

1 | **2**
3

<table>
4 | 5
6 | 7
</table>

4 | 5

6 | 7

The Cavendish

SKILL LEVEL ▼ ▼ ▼ ▼ ▼

NUMBER OF STEPS **8**

HOW TO WEAR IT

YOUR BUILD AVERAGE

COLLAR WIDTH MEDIUM

FABRIC DENSITY AVERAGE

TIE LENGTH AVERAGE

Discovered by Thomas Fink and Yong Mao at the Cavendish Laboratory at Cambridge University in the late 1990s, this is the youngest knot in these pages. (Later knots, not included, look gimmicky because they embrace complexity for complexity's sake.) This knot looks a bit like the ubiquitous Four-in-Hand, but it has more presence. The Cavendish has roughly the same bulk as the Windsor but with a more triangular, slightly asymmetrical shape. Unlike other more substantial knots, the Cavendish works well both with narrower and spread collars.

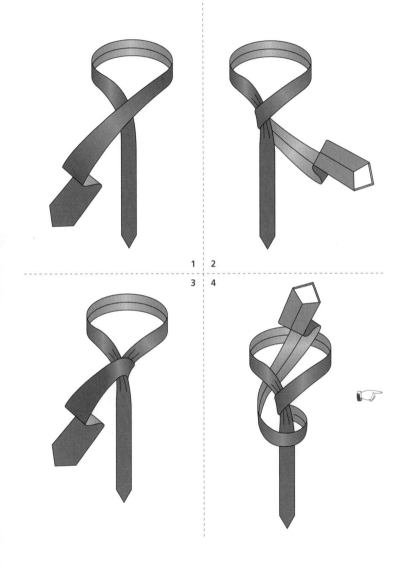

5 | 6
7 | 8

The Plattsburgh

SKILL LEVEL ▼ ▼ ▼ ▼ ▼

NUMBER OF STEPS **8**

HOW TO WEAR IT

YOUR BUILD AVERAGE

COLLAR WIDTH MEDIUM

FABRIC DENSITY AVERAGE

TIE LENGTH AVERAGE

Sometimes called the Dovorian (the demonym for Dover), the Plattsburgh creates a particularly pleasing hourglass shape in the finished tie. Unlike its cousin, the St. Andrew, it looks perfectly symmetrical. Use this knot to breathe new life and strength into a favorite but timeworn tie in your wardrobe.

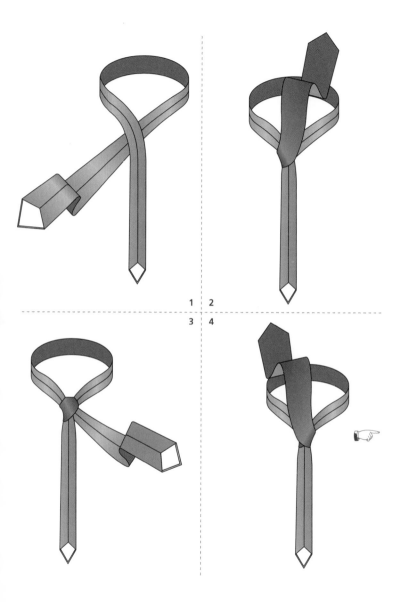

▶ *Illustrations as in Mirror* ◀   69

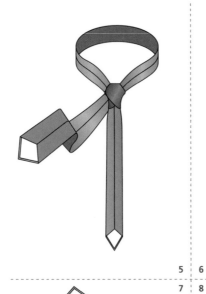

5 | 6
7 | 8

▶ HOW TO TIE A TIE ◀

The St. Andrew

- -

SKILL LEVEL ▼ ▼ ▼ ▼ ▽

NUMBER OF STEPS **8**

- -

HOW TO WEAR IT

YOUR BUILD AVERAGE

COLLAR WIDTH MEDIUM

FABRIC DENSITY AVERAGE

TIE LENGTH AVERAGE

- -

This knot that pays homage to the patron saint of Scotland looks more symmetrical than the Four-in-Hand. When complete, it sets larger than the Half-Windsor but smaller than the Full Windsor, making it a great way to create a more substantial knot with a slightly longer tie made of thinner fabric. It also dimples well.

NOTE: Begin with the tie wrapped inside out, seam showing, around your neck.

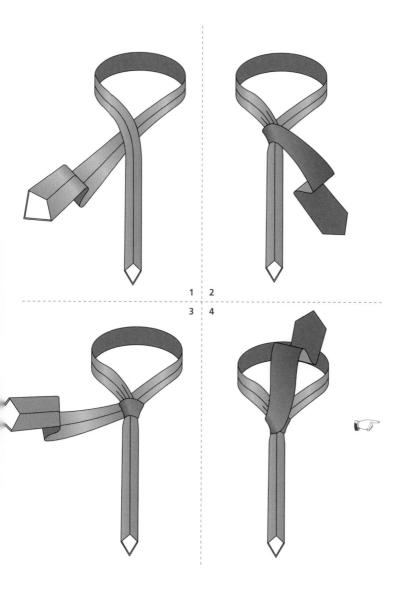

1   2

3   4

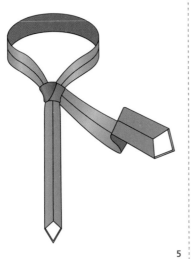

5 | 6

7 | 8

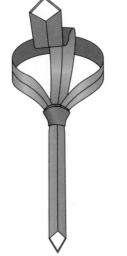

⑭

The Windsor

- -

SKILL LEVEL ▼ ▼ ▼ ▼ ▽
NUMBER OF STEPS **9**

- -

HOW TO WEAR IT

YOUR BUILD LARGER
COLLAR WIDTH WIDER
FABRIC DENSITY THINNER
TIE LENGTH LONGER

- -

1

I n the early 1930s, the always-fashionable prince of Wales (later King Edward VIII) began wearing his neckties tied with particularly large knots. Style watchers noted this dashing new trend and popularized the Windsor knot, which they believed he preferred. After he abdicated the throne in 1936, his younger brother King George VI created the dukedom of Windsor for him, but the duke of Windsor never wore his ties in the knot named for his family. He used a Four-in-Hand with particularly thick ties, which gave the appearance of a Windsor knot. In the 1960s, Lord Lichfield even snapped the duke in a series of how-to photos demonstrating that he didn't use the Windsor knot.

The Windsor—sometimes called a Full Windsor to distinguish it from the Half-Windsor—is the largest of the more common knots still used today. Some consider it slightly old-fashioned, but it will make you look more stylish than its half-brother or the duke's standard Four-in-Hand. Always wear it with a dimple.

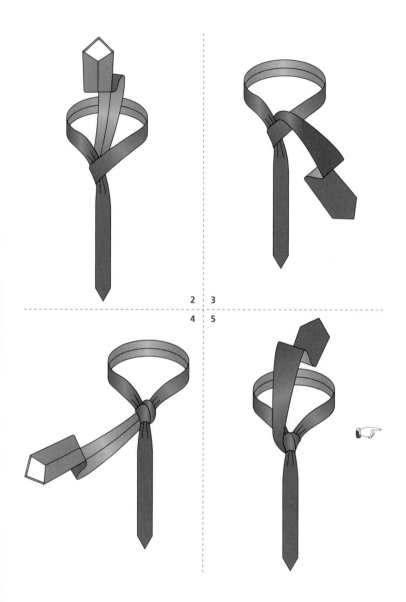

▶ *Illustrations as in Mirror* ◀   77

6 | **7**

8 | **9**

The Murrell

SKILL LEVEL ▼ ▼ ▼ ▼ ▼
NUMBER OF STEPS **9**

HOW TO WEAR IT

YOUR BUILD LARGER
COLLAR WIDTH WIDER
FABRIC DENSITY THINNER
TIE LENGTH LONGER

B rent Murrell invented this
whimsical configuration in 1995
by inverting the Windsor. This unusual
tie makes a bold statement in that it
finishes with the tail hanging *in front
of* the blade rather than behind it,
making it look like your tie is wearing
a tie. Wear this lighthearted look
only for casual occasions and stick to
monochromatic ties so that the knot
rather than the placement of any motif
or pattern holds center stage. Also
consider wearing a vest so that the
tail placement doesn't look like you
dressed yourself in the dark.

NOTE: In the last step, pull the *blade*
to tighten the final knot.

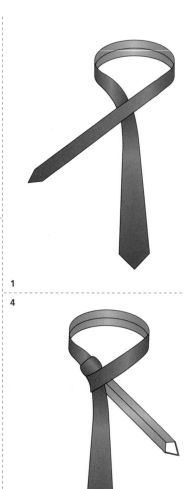

1

4

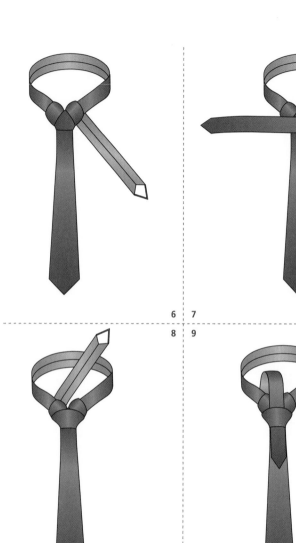

6 7
8 9

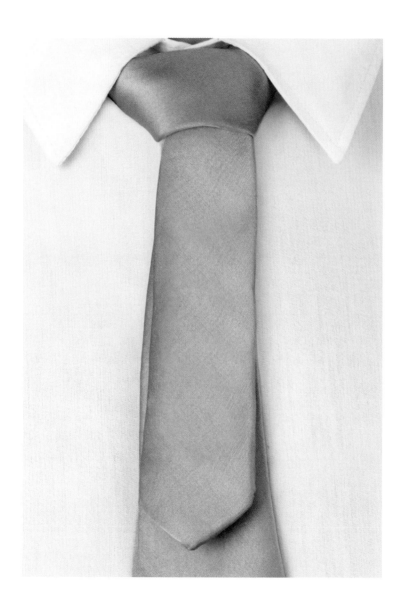

⑯

The Van Wijk

- -

SKILL LEVEL ▼ ▼ ▼ ▼ ▽
NUMBER OF STEPS **9**

- -

HOW TO WEAR IT
YOUR BUILD LARGER
COLLAR WIDTH AVERAGE
FABRIC DENSITY THINNER
TIE LENGTH LONGER

- -

Lisa van Wijk invented this sculptural variant of the Prince Albert as a way to create a more vertically oriented finished knot. When complete, this tall and slender configuration presents an eye-catching visual echo that can work well with striped patterns, and it nicely balances rounder faces. By the same token, avoid this knot if you have a longer, thinner face.

1

4

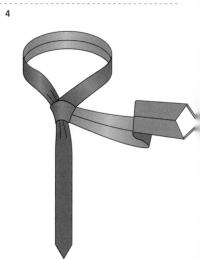

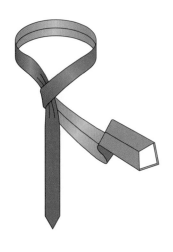

2 | 3

5

6 | 7
8 | 9

The Christensen

- -

SKILL LEVEL ▼ ▼ ▼ ▼ ▼
NUMBER OF STEPS **9**

- -

HOW TO WEAR IT

YOUR BUILD **LARGER**
COLLAR WIDTH **WIDER**
FABRIC DENSITY **THINNER**
TIE LENGTH **LONGER**

In 1917, Stralin and Persson, a Swedish mail order company, included an uncommon looking knot configuration in one of its catalogs, but the publication didn't provide instructions on how to achieve the look. Later, Amanda Christensen, which is the tie and handkerchief company that provides neckwear to the Swedish royal family, created this knot to showcase their goods. Sometimes called the Cross knot because of the way one band of fabric crosses over the other, this method particularly suits skinny ties or narrower with a fixed width.

1

4

2 | 3
5 |

6 | 7
8 | 9

The Grantchester

SKILL LEVEL ▼ ▼ ▼ ▼ ▼
NUMBER OF STEPS **10**

HOW TO WEAR IT
YOUR BUILD LARGER
COLLAR WIDTH WIDER
FABRIC DENSITY THINNER
TIE LENGTH LONGER

Named for the ancient village near Cambridge, England, this configuration continues the Kelvin sequence and mirrors the Four-in-Hand. As a result, it creates a robust yet still appealingly slender finished knot. Use it if you're shorter than average or you want to wear a particularly long tie.

NOTE: Begin with the tie wrapped inside out, seam showing, around your neck.

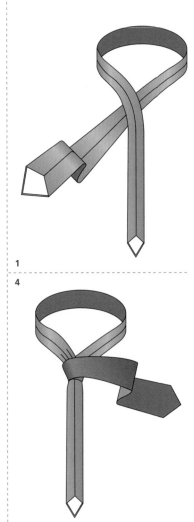

1

4

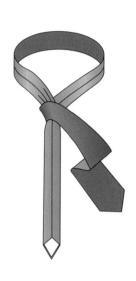

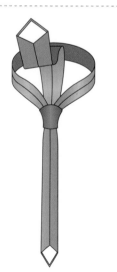

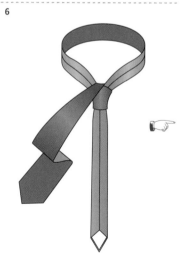

▶ *Illustrations as in Mirror* ◀

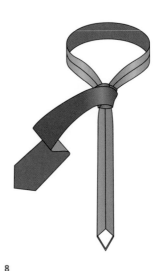

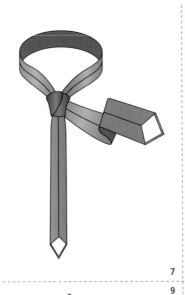

7 | 8
9 | 10

⑲

The Hanover

SKILL LEVEL ▼ ▼ ▼ ▼ ▼
NUMBER OF STEPS **10**

HOW TO WEAR IT

YOUR BUILD	LARGER
COLLAR WIDTH	WIDER
FABRIC DENSITY	THINNER
TIE LENGTH	LONGER

Named for the royal house that ruled Britain for nearly two centuries—from King George I to Queen Victoria—the Hanover knot extends the natural symmetry of the Kent and the Half-Windsor and, when complete, looks larger than a Windsor knot. It makes for an elegant everyday option for the taller, larger man.

NOTE: Begin with the tie wrapped inside out, seam showing, around your neck.

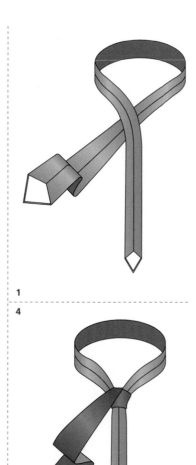

1

4

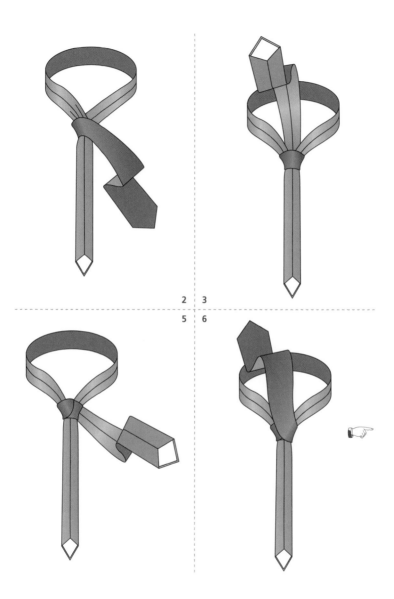

▶ *Illustrations as in Mirror* ◀

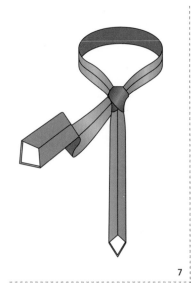

7 | 8

9 | 10

The Trinity

HOW TO WEAR IT

YOUR BUILD	LARGER
COLLAR WIDTH	WIDER
FABRIC DENSITY	THINNER
TIE LENGTH	LONGER

This configuration takes inspiration from Celtic knotwork in general and the triquetra in particular. The finished look can evoke the Holy Trinity of Christianity or your trinity of choice: the Trimurti of Hinduism (Brahma the creator, Vishnu the preserver, and Shiva the destroyer), the Sanxing deities in traditional Chinese religion (Fu representing prosperity, Lu representing status, and Shou representing longevity), or a secular trinity of your own devising, such as three siblings, children, or friends. The final architecture of this knot calls attention to itself, so, if you do want to wear it in a religious context, consider a less formal occasion, such as, in the Christian tradition, an Easter brunch or a church social.

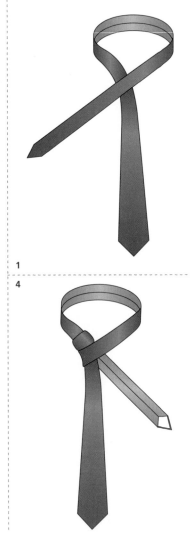

1

4

2 | 3
5 | 6

7 | 8

9 | 10 | 11

HOW TO WEAR IT WELL

A well-tied tie is the first serious step in life.

Oscar Wilde

Fashion is the art of looking good without looking like you tried hard to look good. Most of us have a fairly solid intuition about what to wear and how to wear it, but we don't always trust our instincts or—let's be honest, gentlemen—sometimes they get a little rusty. When it comes to neckwear, more often than not the problem is relatively simple: You just don't have enough ties or the right ties to go with the shirts or suits that you own. Assembling a basic tie wardrobe that suits your needs will eliminate much last-minute angst and frenzy. Learning how to match your ties to your shirts and jackets is the first and most important step, but you also should familiarize yourself with the constellation of necktie accessories and complements even if you never wear them—which is probably a good idea because in men's fashion less is more.

HOW MANY TIES DO YOU NEED?

Every man should own at least one tie. If you're going to own just one, make it a solid silk tie in a dark color: black, charcoal, or navy. The most versatile tie of all is a black knit-silk tie. It works equally well with a bespoke suit or jeans and a dress shirt. In this instance, however, versatility is overrated. While you might get away with this approach, you run the risk of looking stingy or, worse, lacking imagination.

FUN FACT
The average American man owns 7.2 ties.

One tie technically might get the job done, but not having the right basics can mean forcing ties with ill matching shirts and jackets, looking odd, and feeling insecure. Even if you wear ties infrequently, it's best to own a few for different occasions and seasons. A safe handful includes a few solids in dark or versatile colors such as black, blue, red, or purple; one or two with diagonal or "rep" stripes; and some classic all-over patterns. If you prefer less-traditional colors and patterns, adapt accordingly—but make sure your wardrobe already accommodates bolder or more whimsical hues and prints. For the fabric, stick with silk, and you'll be fine. If you want to branch out, consider a cotton tie for summer or a wool tie for winter.

FUN FACT

A person who collects ties is called a grabatologist.

Changing your tie is the easiest, least expensive way to vary your style. If you wear a tie every day or every workday, you really need to have at least one tie for each shirt in your closet. Start with a baker's dozen, but even that number might lead to unwanted repetition. There's nothing

wrong with regularly donning an outfit that looks good on you, but you don't want to be the guy who always wears the same clothes. Plus, your ties will last longer if you give them a breather between wearings. The best option is to have a *couple* of distinctly different ties for each shirt. Again, go mainly for silk and a few in other natural fabrics and in classic colors and patterns. For variety, make the second tie for each shirt a little more interesting, such as a subtle floral print in a secondary color or a slightly bolder stripe. Your shirts and suits will dictate how adventurous you can go. If your shirts are mostly white or pale, solid colors, you can pair them with lots of different ties, both traditional and more daring. Likewise, blue and gray suits can handle lots of different tie colors. If you own a lot of patterned shirts or suits, your tie wardrobe will need to look a bit more conservative for balance.

WHEN TO WEAR A TIE

Some professions still mandate a daily suit and tie, but the rise of the dot-com industry and the informality of coder and creative cultures eliminated a lot of those traditions. If you're not sure, read the room and do as you see. A quick visual survey at the office will tell you when you should wear a tie and when it's OK to skip it.

Some events and social situations also still require you to wear a tie, such as black-tie or white-tie functions or those requiring morning dress. Some private clubs and restaurants enforce a coat-and-tie dress code, further mortifying the unaware by offering those dreaded in-house loaners. In most situations, you can rely on sensibility or observation. If it doesn't seem clear, don't worry. Notions of when to wear a tie differ from West Coast to East, America to Europe, and day to night. Focus on the overall tenor of the gathering. Then wear a tie that you like that goes with your outfit. Confidence looks good on everyone.

NECKTIE COORDINATION

You've bought well-made ties that you know how to knot and that coordinate with your clothes, so now it's time to get down to the nitty-gritty: which tie to wear with which shirt, jacket, or suit. Unfortunately there's no exact science to coordinating them; it's an art. Let observation, instinct, practice, and the confirmation of success by loved ones and colleagues guide you. If your tie collection adheres to the guidelines in this book, you've won half the battle already. A quick perusal of your wardrobe should turn up a tie that will work. Beyond that, keep in mind just a couple of points to look your best.

- ▸ Match your tie to your outfit— first the shirt, then the jacket or suit—*not* your outfit to the tie.
- ▸ Dress for the occasion first and then the weather (not the season).

These two simple considerations will determine what fabrics, colors, and patterns will work best for you. Here are some additional guidelines.

Fabric

Different fabrics denote more or less formality. A good general rule of thumb is that the softer the fabric, the fancier the tie. Woven silk is as formal as a straight tie gets. Printed silk, depending on the pattern, can work with less formal or casual looks. Save rougher fabrics, such as cotton or wool, for a more easygoing outfit. In each case, make sure the textures of the jacket, shirt, and tie fabrics make sense together. A rough tweed jacket looks odd when paired with a woven-silk tie; a heavy winter suit doesn't work with a lightweight cotton tie; and never wear a luxe silk suit with a nubby knitted-wool tie.

This handy infographic indicates which fabrics work best for which climates.

colder	neutral	warmer

LEATHER WOOL POPLIN SILK COTTON LINEN

Color

Common sense and a good look around will tell you a lot about which colors to pair and which combinations to avoid. Darker, muted hues suit serious, more formal occasions and make an obvious choice for fall and winter looks. Brighter, bolder colors look better in warm climates and for more casual outfits. Earth tones, neutrals, and pastels are flexible and can look casual or elegant. Using one of the color principles (families, complements, or opposites, pages 19 and 20), color-match the tie with the shirt first and then the jacket. The whole tie doesn't have to match the shirt or suit color

as long as it contains the right shade of the color you want to emphasize. Monochromatic ensembles—solid-color tie on same-color solid shirt— rarely work and can make you look staid or drab.

Patterns

Motifs become more formal as they grow smaller. For example, a diminutive dot or subtle stripe automatically looks fancier than a big dot or bold stripe. The easiest way to wear a patterned tie is with a solid shirt. By the same token, it's usually a breeze to match a solid tie with a patterned shirt. When you want to mix it up, do so with care.

MIXOLOGY

Despite what you may have heard, you *can* mix different patterns successfully. You just have to know the rule, which is simple: Follow the principle of opposites. When mixing patterns, always select opposing patterns and opposing scales. Never mix two different kinds of stripes or two different geometrics, and never match a small pattern with another small pattern or a large pattern with another large pattern. Also make sure that they don't track

Consider the Collar

Narrower face, narrower collar, smaller knot. Broader face, wider collar, bigger knot. Again, always match your tie to your shirt rather than the other way around. You can take off your tie later, but you can't take off your shirt.

PARTS OF A COLLAR

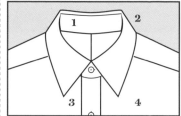

each other (run perpendicularly) creating a jarring basket-weave effect. To seal the union, make sure that the two patterns have a color or feature in common to tie them together, and you're good to go.

THE RIGHT KNOT

Some ties you should wear only with certain shirts, and some knots work better with some collars than with others. The fabric and length of the tie also affect how well it works with a particular shirt and collar. Let's take a closer look.

1. **BAND:** the entire piece of fabric that wraps around your neck
2. **HEIGHT:** the vertical measure of a collar as it fits on your neck
3. **SPREAD:** the distance between the two points
4. **POINTS:** the tips of the collar

STRAIGHT POINT (CLASSIC)

The points of this collar run longer than the points of other collars, though different versions come in different lengths. This shirt always looks great with a tie and can work well with pretty much any knot.

BUTTON-DOWN

On this collar, the points button directly to the shirt to keep them in place. This is a more casual, sporty style. The buttons prevent the wind from blowing the points out of place.

HIDDEN BUTTON-DOWN

This variation features buttons on the underside of the points that affix to the shirt, so you can wear it in more formal situations than the regular Button-Down.

EYELET

More sophisticated than the Tab collar, this style requires a collar bar or pin, which slightly lifts the finished knot and calls a lot of attention to your neck. Wear it only with unshakable confidence. Smaller knots work better with this collar.

TAB

For this type of collar—*always* worn with a tie—the tab between the points supports the knotted tie and gives it a more formal look. Only a small knot will go with this collar.

CLUB (ROUND)

The privileged classes in England favored this unusual collar, which has rounded points, particularly in the 1920s. It looks good on a man with a long face, and it goes well with smaller knots.

SEMI-SPREAD

This collar looks less vertical and stiff than a Straight Point but doesn't set as wide as the full Spread, which makes it a great option for lots of different types of ties and knots.

SPREAD

The spread of this collar sets wider than most, and the band usually feels stiffer than the Straight Point. Always pair the Spread with a larger knot that fills the space between the points.

CUTAWAY

This exceptionally broad collar has foreshortened points, which requires wearing the largest of knots with it.

WINGTIP

This is the collar for black-tie and white-tie events. Wear it only with a bow tie.

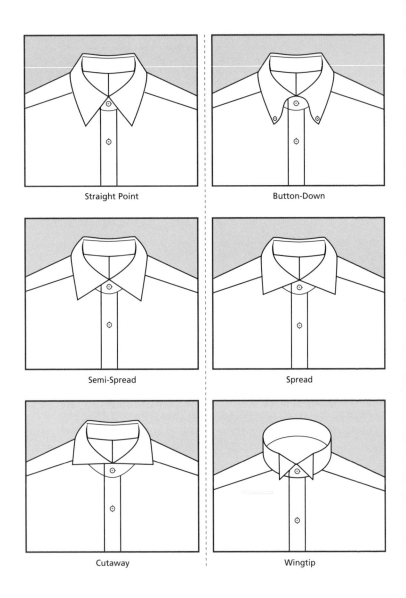

Straight Point

Button-Down

Semi-Spread

Spread

Cutaway

Wingtip

Wearing a Bow Tie

For formal wear, always wear a solid color: white with waistcoat and tails, black with a tuxedo, and always made of silk or brocade and hand-tied. If not black, keep it dark: navy or midnight blue. Elegant stripes, minuscule checks or dots, or a subtle paisley can work, but they push the envelope for formal events. Save more strongly patterned bow ties for more casual events. Avoid large-motif patterns altogether, particularly flora and fauna.

The bow tie should set narrower than your eyes, neck, and collar points. Most bow ties come in a standard size. If you come across one that's much bigger or smaller, stay away. An oversized Butterfly will make you look like Bozo the Clown. A teeny bow tie will make you look like Porky Pig.

Some deviation from the rules is permissible, but, where bow ties are concerned, it's better to follow the rules than to break them.

Other Considerations

▸ The width of your straight tie should match the width of your lapels.

▸ If you're a larger guy, choose a wider, longer tie that will allow for a larger knot, such as the Windsor, Grantchester, or Hanover. Avoid smaller ties and smaller knots, which will make you look even bigger.

▸ If you're a smaller guy, go for a thinner, shorter tie and a smaller knot, such as the Kent, Prince Albert, or Kelvin. Avoid bigger ties and bigger knots, which will make you look even smaller.

▸ When knotted and worn properly, the tie's point should touch the top of your belt buckle but never fall below it. If a tie is too long,

use a more complicated knot, which will use up the extra fabric. Also try starting the knot with the two ends closer together. If you have a short tie, use a simpler knot and try starting the knot with the tail higher on your chest.

▸ A good vest can hide a multitude of sins.

ACCESSORIES

A good tie doesn't need bells or whistles. Each addition to it will more likely than not make it look *less* fashionable. Exceptions occur, as noted below.

Bars, Chains, Clips, Pins + Tacks

All of these accessories keep a tie in its place. Tiepins debuted in the early 1800s, anchoring the many folds of elaborately tied ascots. Initially unadorned pins, they became more extravagant as fashions altered. Now they come in conservative, elaborate, and whimsical variations. A tie tack—a shorter version with a pinch-clasp backing—offers a more modern version

of the tiepin. Both have fallen out of style, and both poke small, permanent holes in your ties. Some menswear aficionados like that a tie chain moors the tie and hangs decoratively across the front—but excessive accessorizing usually looks tacky. Tie chains are to ties what chinstraps are to hats.

Tie bars and clips, by contrast, do look good. These small, oblong bars, worn low on the tie, sometimes feature a clip on the back that holds the tie in place. Look closely when picking one out, though, because some have small rows of teeth that can eat into and damage the fabric of a tie. Select a classic shape in a classic color—sterling silver or gold—and steer clear of any newfangled tie clip fashions, which fall out of fashion as soon as they arrive.

Pocket Squares

These small squares of fabric made especially for suit-jacket pockets look dated these days, but both older and younger men still sometimes wear them. Any man, if he does it right, can wear one well. It should have a texture different from but complementary to the tie. Most natural fabrics—wool, silk, cotton, linen—will work well in this subtle opposition. A colored pocket square should harmonize with

but not exactly match the tie's color and pattern. For best effect, tuck the pocket square loosely in the pocket rather than carefully folding it. Only a thin strip or a few shallow points should show above the pocket line.

Cummerbunds

A cummerbund—from the Persian words for "waist" and "band"—always matches the bow tie in color and material, and the pleats always point upward.

TIE ETIQUETTE

A man may engage in a variety of activities while wearing a tie, but a gentleman never does the following with his ties.

No tucking

Neither between your belt buckle and your pants nor inside your pants. When wearing a seatbelt or similar, the safety device goes *under* the tie so that the tie doesn't crease during the ride.

No tossing

Some diners, rather than taking care while eating, make a great show of throwing their ties over one shoulder in a breezy moment of insouciance. They look as sloppy as the spills they're trying to avoid.

No loosening

Unless you're in the process of removing the tie, it should never look loosened. Either leave it on or take it off where no one can see you undressing. Always loosen the knot in the reverse order that you tied it. Never yank the tail through the knot, which may damage the fabric.

᛫ılı |ıı᛫

HOW TO CARE FOR YOUR TIES

There is no time, sir, at which ties do not matter.

P. G. Wodehouse

Once you've put time, energy, and money into creating a respectable tie wardrobe, you want your ties to last. Owning ties of high quality greatly increases the chances that they'll wear well over a longer period of time. No tie lasts forever, though, and evolving tastes in color, pattern and style have rendered most ties obsolete. Nevertheless, a properly maintained, classic tie will keep you looking your best for a good long while.

WEAR

With the exception of knitted silk, never knot a silk tie too tightly. You might think a taut knot will hold better, but it won't. What it will do—if you do it repeatedly—is strain the fabric, making tiny rips and tears in it. At the end of the day, undo it properly: ease the tail end *gently* through the knot, undo the knot completely, and immediately hang up the tie. Only by hanging will the tie regain its shape and resist wrinkling, both immediately and over time.

It should go without saying, but don't wear the same tie two days in a row. Apart from looking uncouth, the practice will exhaust your ties before their time has come. Let a tie rest for at least two or three days before pressing it back into service.

CLEANING + PRESSING

What to do with a silk tie sidelined by a stain or rumpled seemingly beyond repair? Silk stains easily, and some stains never entirely disappear. Field reports offer no absolute consensus. One school of thought suggests sending the tie to a dry cleaner; another rules that no tie ever should go to a dry cleaner, which surely will ruin it. Some men never have their ties cleaned. They simply wear them until the first sign of shabbiness or an irreversible stain appears, and out they go. For the rest of us, these simple guidelines will help keep your ties clean and wrinkle-free.

If you stain your tie with something greasy, such as fatty food or lipstick, or dark, such as red wine or ink, it's probably best to salute your old friend and say goodbye. With a milder stain, you can try dabbing a tiny bit of water on the spot and *gently* rubbing the stained fabric against itself or using a slightly damp cloth to do the same. If that valiant effort doesn't work, you have a couple of options. If you live in a major urban center, take the tie to a specialty dry cleaning service that deals exclusively with ties. In the Chelsea neighborhood of New York City, for example, Tiecrafters offers a tie's best hope for resurrection. Otherwise, take the tie to the best dry cleaner you can find. Better dry cleaners often advertise that they "specialize" in ties, which may or may not be true, but you're safer with this approach than risking the garment with any old cleaner.

Don't try to get the spot out with commercial stain remover or club soda. Ties also never go in a washing machine—not the one at home nor one at a professional laundry service. Likewise, you mustn't hand-wash them. These approaches may remove a stain, but they also will shrink parts of the garment disproportionately.

Ironing your ties is also generally a bad idea. One relatively safe way to use steam to remove creases is to boil a kettle of water and then hold the wrinkles into the water vapor to relax them. In a messy pinch, you can go heavy on the steam button and iron the garment directly, but don't make a habit of this practice. At best, it will wear out the tie more quickly. At worst, you'll wind up with scorched neckwear. Also be careful how you

iron because an absolutely flat tie won't hang properly when you put it back on.

You can buy a tie press, which works for ties made of silk and other heat-abhorrent materials. If a tie press sounds extravagant or unnecessary, here's an alternative method. If the tie has more wrinkles than a night's hang or a kettle steam will cure, turn on your shower as hot as it goes. Drape the tie over a hanger and hang it opposite from the shower head, beyond the water's reach. Leave it there for ten to twenty minutes. Remove the tie and lay it flat on a bureau or counter to dry, and you'll be good to go.

STORAGE

The best place to hang your ties at home is in a closet because darkness slows the fabric's natural fading process. Tie racks allow you to hang multiple ties lengthwise, which is great because the ties stay put all in one place. Your next best bet is a regular old hanger with a crossbar. Drape the tie evenly over the crossbar so that it doesn't slip off, and you're done. If you can't hang your ties, lay them flat in a drawer. Always store knitted ties flat or carefully rolled in

a drawer to prevent them from bagging and stretching disproportionately.

When traveling, you also have a couple of options. The proper method calls for a dedicated tie bag or case that allows the ties to lie flat and secures them with horizontal straps. Such a case or bag will tuck easily into your suitcase and keep the ties in more or less immaculate condition. If a tie case sounds extreme or profligate, the old standby works perfectly well. Roll the ties in loose coils and pop them in your shoes, close enough together so they don't unroll, while taking care not to squish them. They should look good as new when you unpack.

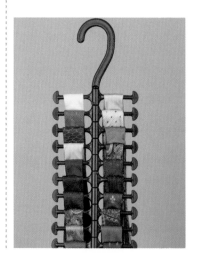

OTHER NECKWEAR

Oh I have been to Ludlow fair
and left my necktie God knows where.

A. E. Housman

The kind of tie you wear says a lot about you. Again, as with dinner party conversation or workplace chitchat, less is more. You're more likely to impress people by saying less about yourself and your fashion sense. But some neckwear choices shout, "Look at me!" Why should you care? Well, that's the point. Maybe you shouldn't. Notable titans of industry and the arts have stepped out in idiosyncratic style, including Oscar Wilde and Aristotle Onassis. An eccentric tie alone won't land you on the cover of a magazine, but it never hurts to know your options.

ASCOT

This smallish scarf worn loosely tied around the neck and tucked into a shirt takes its name from England's renowned horse racing event, at which it remains required wear for

men, along with top hat and tails. It descends from the cravat and proved very popular in the latter part of the nineteenth century among men of the middle and upper classes, who wore it most often with a tiepin. The rise of the straight tie rendered the ascot practically extinct, except for rare functions that call for morning

dress. Exceptionally few men have to own morning dress, so, if you find yourself in need, you can rent it from a serious formal-wear or menswear outfitter. If you forego the pre-tied version, shop staff will show you how to tie the ascot.

Men who can wear an ascot well tend to be iconically astute (Sherlock Holmes), devilishly charming (David Niven), or arrestingly handsome (Cary Grant). As a group, they almost always are over the age of 45 and usually have some dignified silver in their hair. Let that be a lesson to you.

BANDANNA

We think of the bandanna as a totem of the American West, but the word comes from Sanskrit and literally means tie-dyed cloth. Imported in the early eighteenth century from India to England and America, the bandanna began as a silk kerchief in vivid hues, the first brightly colored necktie that Westerners wore. British boxer James Belcher wore a brightly patterned neckerchief that popularized the style around the same time that Beau Brummell was flaunting his cravats. For reasons of practicality and expense, the bandanna evolved into its present cotton form, and today it goes hand in hand with the culture of cowboys, railroad workers, and other American pioneers. Because of that working-class tradition, the bandanna—often worn in much the same way as the ascot—doesn't signal the same level of pretense. If you want to try the look, wear it with a cotton shirt, knot it like a kerchief or cross, and tuck it loosely in your shirt.

BOLO

The story goes that Arizona cowboy Victor Cedarstaff invented this odd piece of neckwear in the 1940s, when, on the range, the wind blew his hat off his head. Worried about losing the decorative hatband, he placed it around his neck, and the idea for a sliding necktie struck him. He fashioned it after

NECK SLIP

This esoteric garment, a hybrid of the straight tie and the ascot, is worn looped and tucked in a loose knot, with the front, arrow-shaped end tucked into the front of the shirt. Usually worn with a smoking jacket, it belongs to the golden age of horror films. The most recent sighting places it on Vincent Price at a series of poolside cocktail parties in Hollywood, circa 1960.

STRING TIE

This narrow strip of cotton or velvet tied so the tails hang over the wearer's chest began life more or less as a Southern version of a bow tie. Elvis Presley wore one reasonably well, but that was another time—and he was Elvis. Harland Sanders famously wore one as the brand ambassador for his fried-chicken empire, and, for the sake of posterity, we should let him have the look.

the *bolas*, a two-headed throwing weapon popular with gauchos in South America for dropping game by the legs. The look caught on, and Cedarstaff filed a patent for it in 1954. Around the same time, fashionable young Brits called Teddy Boys took a shine to the tie, which they called a Slim Jim. The bolo became Arizona's official neckwear in 1971, and New Mexico and Texas followed suit in 2007, making it a distinctly Southwestern look.

INDEX

IMAGE CREDITS

TIE TABLE

Knot	Skill Level	Steps	Your Build	Collar Width	Fabric Density	Tie Length	Page
Kent	▼▽▽▽▽	3	▼▽▽	▼▽▽	▼▼▼	▼▽▽	28
Prince Albert	▼▽▽▽▽	4	▼▽▽	▼▽▽	▼▼▼	▼▽▽	30
Four-in-Hand	▼▽▽▽▽	5	▼▽▽	▼▽▽	▼▼▼	▼▽▽	32
Kelvin	▼▼▽▽▽	5	▼▽▽	▼▽▽	▼▼▼	▼▽▽	36
Pratt	▼▼▽▽▽	6	▼▽▽	▼▼▽	▼▼▼	▼▽▽	40
Nicky	▼▼▽▽▽	6	▼▼▽	▼▼▽	▼▼▼	▼▼▼	44
Diagonal	▼▼▽▽▽	6	▼▼▽	▼▼▽	▼▼▼	▼▼▼	48
Bow Tie	▼▼▼▼▽	7	all	▼▼▽	▼▼▽	▼▼▼	52
Atlantic	▼▼▼▽▽	7	▼▼▽	▼▼▽	▼▼▽	▼▼▽	56
Half-Windsor	▼▼▼▽▽	7	▼▼▽	▼▼▽	▼▼▽	▼▼▽	60
Cavendish	▼▼▼▽▽	7	▼▼▽	▼▼▽	▼▼▽	▼▼▽	64
Plattsburgh	▼▼▼▽▽	8	▼▼▽	▼▼▽	▼▼▽	▼▼▽	68
St. Andrew	▼▼▼▼▽	8	▼▼▽	▼▼▽	▼▼▽	▼▼▽	72
Windsor	▼▼▼▼▽	9	▼▼▼	▼▼▼	▼▽▽	▼▼▼	76
Murrell	▼▼▼▼▽	9	▼▼▼	▼▼▼	▼▽▽	▼▼▼	80
Van Wijk	▼▼▼▼▽	9	▼▼▼	▼▼▼	▼▽▽	▼▼▼	84
Christensen	▼▼▼▼▼	9	▼▼▼	▼▼▼	▼▼▽	▼▼▼	88
Grantchester	▼▼▼▼▼	10	▼▼▼	▼▼▼	▼▼▽	▼▼▼	92
Hanover	▼▼▼▼▼	10	▼▼▼	▼▼▼	▼▽▽	▼▼▼	96
Trinity	▼▼▼▼▼	11	▼▼▼	▼▼▼	▼▽▽	▼▼▼	100